BUSES IN GREATER LONDON

PETER TUCKER

Front cover: A ubiquitous MCW Metrobus crosses Westminster Bridge in October 1999 bound for Streatham station.

Back cover: The AEC Routemaster is the archetypal London bus. WLT 871, new in 1962, pauses at Strand in 2014.

First published 2024

Amberley Publishing
The Hill, Stroud
Gloucestershire, GL5 4EP

www.amberley-books.com

Copyright © Peter Tucker, 2024

The right of Peter Tucker to be identified as the Author of this work has been asserted in accordance with the Copyrights, Designs and Patents Act 1988.

ISBN 978 1 3981 1666 5 (print)
ISBN 978 1 3981 1667 2 (ebook)

All rights reserved. No part of this book may be reprinted or reproduced or utilised in any form or by any electronic, mechanical or other means, now known or hereafter invented, including photocopying and recording, or in any information storage or retrieval system, without the permission in writing from the Publishers.

British Library Cataloguing in Publication Data.
A catalogue record for this book is available from the British Library.

Origination by Amberley Publishing.
Printed in the UK.

Appointed GPSR EU Representative: Easy Access System Europe Oü, 16879218
Address: Mustamäe tee 50, 10621, Tallinn, Estonia
Contact Details: gpsr.requests@easproject.com, +358 40 500 3575

Introduction

Buses in Greater London is a photographic survey of London's red buses, give or take a few exceptions, between 1993 and early 2023. The area featured in this book is conterminous with the thirty-two boroughs that constitute Greater London today. These include Barking & Dagenham, City of Westminster, Harrow, Merton, Tower Hamlets, Waltham Forest and Wandsworth. The boroughs are usually named after at least one principal settlement or a place of historic importance. Brent is named after a Middlesex river to avoid giving prominence to Wembley or Willesden. Redbridge was named after a bridge despite the presence of Ilford, a major commercial centre. Fulham was added to Hammersmith to become Hammersmith & Fulham on 1 January 1979.

Greater London was established in 1965 ahead of the later metropolitan counties. The new Greater London Council (GLC) used the old London County Council, formed on 21 March 1889, as a starting point. The remainder of Greater London came at the expense of those areas known as London over the Border (Acton, Leyton, Tottenham, West Ham, etc.) or Metroland (Edgware, Harrow, Northwood, Wembley, etc.). Large portions of Essex, Kent, Surrey and part of Hertfordshire were annexed by the GLC. In reality, the influence of London on neighbouring counties was already significant. London Transport operated well into the Home Counties, the underground reached as far as Amersham, Epping and Watford and many towns such as Dagenham, Edgware and Ilford were inextricably linked with London.

The creation of Greater London meant the death knell for Middlesex, the county of the middle Saxons. Most of the county, an area encompassing Brentford, Enfield, Harrow, Uxbridge and at one time the East End, disappeared into the new Greater London Council. Middlesex was abolished in 1965, and what was not annexed by the GLC was transferred to Hertfordshire or Surrey.

The Greater London Council was controversially dissolved in 1986, the boroughs becoming unitary authorities. Recognising the need for a strategic authority, Labour inaugurated the Greater London Authority (GLA) in 2000 following a successful referendum in May 1998. A unique innovation by British standards, the devolved GLA works in cooperation with London's thirty-two boroughs and the City of London Corporation. The face of the GLA is the Mayor of London, the first being Ken Livingstone, who stood as an independent candidate after a spat with the Labour Party. The Mayor of London has a significant profile, especially as far as buses are concerned – bendy buses and New Routemasters have been hot political topics in London elections.

Broadly speaking, Greater London is contained within the M25 orbital route with the River Thames dividing the city in two. Greater London encompasses everything from Buckingham Palace, Canary Wharf, Crayford, Downe, Hampton Court Palace, Heathrow Airport, Leyton Orient Football Club, Peckham, St Paul's Cathedral, Theatre Land, Woodford Wells and Wennington Marshes – the link of course is the familiar red bus or underground train.

London's suburbs are fascinating from a social and historical perspective and make interesting terrain for a study of public transport or domestic architecture. The Metroland suburbs of Brent, Harrow and Hillingdon tell us much about the values of the aspiring middle classes they were built for. Numerous underground stations and shopping parades have interesting period details that are in danger of being irreparably damaged or destroyed forever. Sometime in the future suburbs like Kingsbury and Sudbury will be back in vogue. Art-deco legacies such as Perivale's Hoover building (now a Tesco store) and underground stations such as Arnos Grove are an essential part of London's architectural fabric. Inner London can be in turns hideously ugly, run down or absolutely charming – often in the space of several hundred yards. While the merits of brutalist post-war structures such as Balfron Tower (Poplar) are hotly debated, they are an inescapable part of the London skyline. The flip side of Metroland, the monstrous post-war housing schemes tell us what contempt the town planners had for the working classes. A ride on a bus through London can be revealing and highly rewarding. Turn off the phone and look at the architecture and absorb the culture and history. It's not all good but it is always fascinating.

London remains a paradox; it can't be summed up in one positive or negative word. It can be alternately compelling and dreadful, frenetic and calm, edgy and peaceful, and it is always changing – no London district stays the same for long. London possesses vibrancy like no other British city, and no British city can claim to have so many iconic symbols and places – the London Transport roundel and Abbey Road included. London is the world, England, popular and high culture and so forth in one city. The thought of a visit to London always excites the mind but the experience of being there can soon make one search for a quick exit. In short, London is probably the world's greatest city, warts and all.

The origins of London's buses can be traced back to July 1829 when George Shilibeer began a horse-drawn omnibus service along New Road. The idea was a French one, credited to Stanislas Baudry, who had operated a similar scheme in Nantes and later Paris. A key advantage of Shilibeer's Omnibus over the existing Hackney coaches was the absence of booking arrangements, the ability to pick up and set down passengers on a fixed route and the increased capacity of the coaches.

The arrival of the omnibuses brought severe competition and road congestion. In 1851, there were over 150 omnibus routes in London and numerous operators working together in associations. Thereafter there was a thread of developments and innovations leading to the creation of the London General Omnibus Company (LGOC) in 1856, The London Traffic Act 1924, The London Passenger Transport Act 1933, The Transport (London) Act 1969, The London Regional Transport Act 1984, right through to the privatisation of London Buses in 1994/95. Those wanting a definitive and detailed history of transport in London are recommended to read publications such as John Reed's lucid and succinct *London Buses Past and Present* (Capital Transport, 1988).

The London Regional Transport Act 1984 has a direct connection with the buses we see featured in this book today. The legislation paved the way for the privatisation of London's buses. By 1984, London Transport had already been split into districts including Forest, Leaside and Watling. A key part of the legislation allowed both private operators and London Buses to tender for bus routes within Greater London. Tendering was intended to lower costs, reduce public subsidies, improve efficiency and promote competition in a bid to improve public services.

On 13 July 1985 Len Wright, trading as London Buslines, became the first private contract operator in the capital, having gained service 81 between Hounslow and Slough. Beginning with a fleet of used Daimler Fleetlines, London Buslines continued to expand and was acquired by CentreWest on 20 March 1996 before being phased out as a result of FirstBus ownership from 1997. A notable feature of the tendering process was the controversial decision to allow independent operators to use non-red colours, a policy changed in 1997 to a minimum of 80 per cent red. Today, virtually all buses are in overall red.

Early independent operators of services for London Regional Transport included Boroline Maidstone and Eastern National. Ensignbus of Purfleet is a good example of an independent contractor, the company adopting a bright blue and silver livery and using a mix of new and used stock, including two 'jumbo' Bristol VRs from Reading. Ensign services could be seen around Barking, Cranham, Ilford, Romford and out to Grays in Essex proper. Grey-Green won the highly prestigious contract to operate service 24 (Hampstead–Pimlico) in November 1988, bringing the firm's distinctive livery and new Volvos into the heart of central London. London Buses had mixed fortunes in winning contracts and developing their own subsidiaries. Orpington-based Roundabout was formed in 1986 and helped pioneer the use of minibuses in Greater London. Selkent's low-cost subsidiary Bexleybus (1988–91) was short-lived and beset by industrial strife. A notable feature of the Bexleybus fleet was the application of a distinctive blue and cream livery, far removed from London red. The Stanwell Bus Company (Westlink) formed in 1986 was more successful, eventually becoming part of London United in 1995. London Coaches was an interesting operation launched in 1986 to develop private-hire and sightseeing work. London Buses also developed local brand names such as SuttonBus and Uxbridge Buses while minibuses received catchy titles such as Hoppa or Streetline.

The tendering process was not without difficulties. Some operators found the requirements of timetabling and vehicle maintenance demanding. The recruitment of staff, reliability of buses and traffic congestion was also a problem. Tendering added colour, literally, to the transport scene in London with Kentish Bus, London & Country and Capital Citybus being especially memorable for their vibrant use of paint.

By 1991, London Buses operated the following divisions: CentreWest, East London, Leaside, London Central, London General, London Northern, London United, Metroline, Selkent, South London, Stanwell Bus Company (Westlink) and London Coaches. London Forest ceased trading on 23 November 1991 after troubled labour relations. The forthcoming privatisation was a foregone conclusion.

Between January 1994 and January 1995 the subsidiaries of London Buses Ltd were privatised. Over 5,000 buses passed into private ownership in a sale which netted London Transport and the government over £230 million. Since privatisation various operators have come and gone, including Stagecoach, who pulled out of London for a period but are back today. Several operators are foreign-owned including Arriva and RATP Dev Transit. There is also a far wider variety of bus types than any time before 1986. Keeping abreast of bus fleets is best conducted via the PSV Circle, websites and transport publications; such is the fluidity of the industry in London.

Today, Transport for London (TfL), the successor to London Regional Transport, is responsible for the bulk of public transport in the capital. TfL was formed on 3 July 2000 as a result of the Greater London Authority Act 1999. The Greater London Authority remains in overall charge of TfL. TfL has responsibility for key aspects of London's transport structure including London Underground, London Buses, London Rail, the Elizabeth Line and from as late as 2003 London Underground. Buses are operated by private franchises in a smart red livery with the familiar London roundel logo.

The patronage of buses in London remains an important issue, especially with the Congestion Zone and the controversial Ultra Low Emission Zone. Since the pandemic London's buses have seen a fall in patronage with City Hall axing many routes in a bid to save money. TfL's financial black hole was enough to give most accountants nightmares, the Conservative government ordering the authority to save £730 million per year from 2022. LBC Radio reported in July 2022 the ending of such famous routes as the 16 (Victoria–Cricklewood Bus Garage) and the 24 (Hampstead Heath–Pimlico). Frequency reductions have taken over 300 buses off London's roads since 2020. Buses also face competition from the Docklands Light Railway, TfL Rail, Tramlink but probably not the underused Emirates Air Line cable car linking North Greenwich and the Royal Docks at Newham. In an interesting twist to earlier events, RailTech.com reported in August 2022 the intention of the Conservative government to nationalise Transport for London.

Buses in Greater London is not intended to be a definitive guide to London's buses, routes and history. This aspect has been covered expertly by others in numerous publications. Rather this book aims to provide a snapshot of London's red buses at work in all of the thirty-two boroughs. The book deliberately places more emphasis on the districts outside the Cities of London and Westminster. The photographic journey takes us around some broadly representative areas of London, taking in the centre, inner city, suburbs and rural-urban fringe. Inevitably, it was not possible to include every London district in this book, however all the boroughs are represented, even if briefly. The photographs make no claims to be works of art, just adequate records of London's buses at work.

I would like to thank Thomas Anthony for proofreading the text. Any errors in the book are mine. Enjoy the tour of Greater London!

A quartet of buses at Turnpike Lane bus station during January 2023.

Victoria coach station is a notoriously cramped and hectic terminus in the heart of central London. In Airbus branding, MCW Metrobus M107 prepares to work route A1 to Heathrow Airport during August 1993. The MCW Metrobus was built in Birmingham between 1978 and 1989, London Transport purchasing over 1,400. A small number of Metrobuses were bodied by Alexander and Northern Counties, some of the former later working in London.

The graceful and elegant lines of the AEC Routemaster are an iconic symbol of British culture and design. In a typical London scene, not likely to be repeated, RML 2661 negotiates heavy traffic at Trafalgar Square bound for Marble Arch. The extra central windows are a clue that No. 2661 is a 30 foot long-wheelbase variant, hence the code RML. City of Westminster, August 1994.

A splendid AEC Routemaster, RML 2546, enters Terminus Place, Victoria, during August 1994. The first production Routemasters left the AEC works at Southall in 1958, following the introduction of prototype RM1 in 1956 (built in 1954) and RM2 in 1957 (built in 1955). There were 2,875 built, with all but 115 going to London Transport. The last Routemasters were built in 1968 when single-deckers or rear-engined double-deckers were in vogue. A minority of Routemasters were built with conventional, front entrance doors and there was a rear-engined version, coded FRM1, constructed in 1966.

The original Leyland National, styled by Michelotti, was an advanced design at launch in 1971. The improved National 2 of 1979 was distinguished by a bulbous front and the deletion of the troublesome Leyland 510 engine. Recognising the basic robustness of the National, East Lancs introduced the Leyland National Greenway in 1991, a rebuild option featuring a fresh design and refurbished interior. One of the 176 National Greenways built, GLS 479 is seen at Victoria during August 1994 in Red Arrow branding.

From the bustle of central London to the very edge of the metropolis in the Borough of Richmond-upon-Thames. Leyland Titan T 861, in service with Westlink (Stanwell Bus Company), crosses Hampton Bridge bound for West Molesey, Surrey. In the background and out of shot is the magnificent Hampton Court Palace. The palace was constructed from 1514 for Cardinal Wolsey, the Archbishop of Canterbury. Following Wolsey's fall, the palace passed to Henry VIII, who enlarged it. Wolsey died in disgrace at Leicester Abbey on 29 November 1530. Hampton Court, August 1994.

A hazy scene at Victoria bus station in August 1995. Leaside Buses AEC Routemaster, RML 2682, departs for Clapton Pond via Bloomsbury and Islington. She had been new to London Transport's Hanwell garage. In the background, an unidentified Leaside Buses Routemaster departs for Tottenham. Leaside Buses principal operating area at the time was north London, with the River Lea being a focal point. Besides central London, Leaside buses could be seen at destinations which included Archway, Barnet, Edmonton, Enfield, Walthamstow and Wood Green.

The handsome lines of the Northern Counties Palatine-bodied Volvo Olympian are shown on Stagecoach Selkent VN 174 at Westminster Bridge in October 1999. Selkent stood for South East London and Kent, in the case of Kent, those boroughs such as Bexley and Bromley which were annexed by London in 1965 but carried Kent postcodes. VN 174 was working service 53 to Plumstead Common via Old Kent Road and New Cross. Selkent was acquired by Stagecoach on 6 September 1994.

The use of open-top sightseeing buses in London grew exponentially in the 1990s. Resplendent in Arriva's The Original Tour livery, this 1979 MCW Metrobus was previously in service with Cowie-owned South London. Cowie was rebranded Arriva in 1997, becoming part of Deutsche Bahn in 2010. The Original Tour was founded by London Transport in 1951 to coincide with the Festival of Britain. The division was privatised in 1986 and sold to Arriva in 1997. At the time of writing, RATP Dev. now own the company, which trades as Tootbus London. Parliament Street, October 1999.

The Leyland Titan established itself as one of the key London buses of the 1980s. A sophisticated product, the Titan was beset by production difficulties at the Park Royal works, and market resistance from other bus operators. London Transport purchased 1,164 Titans new, the last being constructed in 1984 at Lillyhall, Workington. Other Titans went to Reading, West Midlands PTE (all sold to London Transport) and Greater Manchester PTE. Workington-built T 709 approaches Trafalgar Square bound for Dulwich in October 1999.

Although AEC Routemaster operation officially ended in 2005, certain heritage journeys continued to use the type until 2021. Stagecoach East London RM 2050 presents a fine sight at Southampton Street en route to Tower Hill in 2014. New in 1964, RM 2050 represents the standard 27-foot 6-inch length Routemaster, probably the most aesthetically pleasing variant. Various reasons have been posited for the end of the heritage Routemasters including the introduction of ULEZ, falling patronage and accessibility issues.

Metroline VW 1288, a Wright-bodied Volvo B9TL, works through central London bound for North Finchley. Margaret Thatcher was MP for Finchley between 1959 and 1992.

Perhaps the most significant, or at least most hyped, bus to enter service in London for decades was the New Routemaster of 2011. Built by Wrightbus, about 1,000 were produced between 2011 and 2017. Time will tell if the New Routemaster, sometimes nicknamed the Borismaster, will hold up against the beloved RT or AEC Routemaster. LTZ 1063 stands at Savoy Street, Strand, on service 11 to Fulham Broadway.

Lacking the characteristic blue and red livery once associated with Metroline, ADL President-bodied Volvo B7TL, VPL 630, moves gingerly along Aldwych on a wet day in early 2014. Aldwych is built upon an Anglo-Saxon settlement known as Lundenwic. Today hotels, restaurants and the High Commissions of Australia and India dominate the area.

Arriva VLA 6 is an Alexander-bodied Volvo B7TL new in 2003. Pictured turning onto Lancaster Place and Waterloo Bridge, it was bound for Penge, one of the less fashionable parts of the London Borough of Bromley. Penge, together with Balham and Neasden, was for years the butt of comedian's jokes.

At the same location Arriva VLA 28 turns onto Lancaster Place, displaying a rather grubby appearance. Dual-door buses have remained in fashion in London, having been a fad in areas like Tyne & Wear during the 1970s. Safety concerns and the potential for illegal loadings having counted against dual-door buses in some provincial areas.

Arriva HV 19 is a Volvo B5L Hybrid with rather heavy looking Wright Gemini 2 bodywork. New in 2010, it was pictured crossing Waterloo Bridge in mid-2014. The bridge was opened in 1942, replacing Rennie's original of 1817. Waterloo Bridge has a rather gruesome history, the murder of Bulgarian dissident Georgi Markov on 7 September 1978 being one of the best-known homicides associated with the location.

A partial shot of Stagecoach No. 17802, a TransBus Trident/TransBus ALX400 new in 2003. Known to most people as an Alexander-bodied Dennis Trident, it was pictured passing young coffee drinkers outside a Starbucks in central London during 2014.

Arriva DW 241, a Wright-bodied VDL Bus DB300, passes the intriguingly titled and typically British Molly Moggs pub en route for Clapton Pond. The Soho bar has since closed and at the time of writing is now the Coach & Horses. Charing Cross Road, 2014.

Two modern updates of London iconography – the red bus and black hackney carriage in central London. On the left, Wright-bodied DW 235 heads for Clapton Pond. On the right is a 2007 London Taxis International cab bound for some unknown destination. The arrival of Uber on the capital's transport scene has been the source of considerable consternation with traditional black-cab drivers. In 2023, Uber was operating in over 10,000 cities worldwide.

A beautifully maintained AEC Routemaster, RM 871, pauses at Somerset House on a Tower Hill–Trafalgar Square heritage route in 2014. RM 871 was new in January 1962 and was operated later in life by both East Yorkshire and Reading Mainline.

In the leafy surroundings of St Giles, part of the London Borough of Camden, Arriva VLA 59 was pictured on layover in 2014. St Giles' best-known landmark is Centre Point, a 385-foot tower block opened in 1964. Controversial from the start, a French equivalent would be Tour Montparnasse, a distinctive, lone tower block in the 15th arrondissement of Paris, standing a lofty 689 feet high.

VWL 39 is a Wright-bodied Volvo B7TL new in 2004 and pictured in service during 2014 with London General. Based at Merton, London General was subject to a management buyout in 1994 before acquisition by the expanding Go-Ahead Group in May 1996. Go-Ahead London is part of the Tyneside-based Go-Ahead Group, formed in 1987 from the former National Bus Company subsidiary Northern General.

Back in the City of Westminster at Strand, modern Routemaster LT 71 pauses at traffic lights bound for Hammersmith. Strand means 'bank' or 'shore', which is appropriate given the road's proximity to the River Thames. The word strand is sometimes used for the wider locality. Other places to use the word strand include Gillingham, Kent and Strand-on-the-Green at Chiswick.

An inconsiderately parked Nissan Micra poses no problem for Arriva HV 87 at Shaftesbury Avenue in 2014. Shaftsbury Avenue was laid out in 1877–86 and is named after the 7th Earl of Shaftsbury. The road is shared between the boroughs of Westminster and Camden, Cambridge Circus forming the boundary point.

Recent building developments in the City of London have been controversial with concerns raised about the design and scale of the structures. Towering over London Bridge, the 'Cheesegrater' and 'Scalpel' make Metroline's Enviro400 look insignificant in this view from London Bridge. Rennie's London Bridge of 1831 was dismantled and reconstructed in Arizona from 1968. London Bridge, 2014.

One of the most familiar double-deck designs in recent times has been the Alexander Dennis Enviro400. At the Old Vic in the London Borough of Lambeth, Metroline's Enviro400 Hybrid THE 1231 is shown from the rear in the summer of 2014. Lambeth stretches as far south as Streatham and includes Brixton, Clapham, Kennington, Stockwell and Vauxhall.

Abellio London No. 9040 is a 2005 Wright-bodied Volvo B7TL captured at Southwark Street, Bankside on service 381 to Peckham. Entertainment (including the original Globe Theatre) and brewing were staple activities at Bankside, an area of Southwark subjected to severe bombing in the Second World War.

A grab shot of the innovative Wright-bodied VDL Bus SB200 LF Fuelcell bus. In plain English, a hydrogen bus operated originally by First London. First started retreating from London in 2007, the final services terminating in September 2013. Southwark, 2014.

With the backdrop of another London pub, The Barrowboy & Banker, Abellio No. 9754 works through Borough, bound for Peckham in early 2014. Borough is the historic commercial centre of Southwark. The modern London Borough of Southwark stretches from the south bank of the Thames to include Bermondsey, Camberwell and Peckham, plus the rising ground around Dulwich.

The Shard is another controversial London skyscraper opened in 2012 and at the time of writing the tallest building in the United Kingdom. Stagecoach Enviro400 No. 12262 passes the structure in 2014 bound for Bellingham. In contrast to Paris, London is extremely liberal in granting permission for the construction of skyscrapers. Most of Paris' skyscrapers are located at La Defense in the Hauts-de-Seine department outside the capital.

London Bridge station at Southwark was opened in 1836 and was extensively rebuilt in the early 1970s. The station, central London's first, was remodelled again in the 2010s and today serves destinations in Kent, London, Surrey and Sussex, plus Bedford, Luton and Peterborough via the Thameslink route. Amid numerous pedestrians, Abellio No. 9054 works towards City Hall on a gloomy winter's day in 2014.

Anybody who watched the popular ITV television series *London's Burning* might recognise this location in Bermondsey. Many episodes were filmed around Bermondsey's Dockhead fire station and the surrounding areas of Southwark and Rotherhithe, plus Lewisham and Woolwich. Stagecoach Selkent No. 18494, an ADL Trident/ADL ALX400 combination, was working service 47 to Shoreditch on the north bank of the Thames. Stagecoach divested itself of Stagecoach London to Macquarie Bank in 2006. By October 2010 East London and Selkent were back in Stagecoach ownership.

Also at Bermondsey is Abellio London No. 2406, an ADL Enviro400 Hybrid working the busy service 188 to North Greenwich. Part of the 1988 film *A Fish Called Wanda* and certain episodes of the television series *Dempsey and Makepeace* were filmed in the Bermondsey area, a district much gentrified since the 1980s.

Deptford is a historic, somewhat hip part of inner south-east London, famous for the docks established by Henry VIII. Playwright Christopher Marlowe was murdered in a pub brawl at Deptford in May 1593. Marlowe's plays include *Tamburlaine*, *Doctor Faustus* and *Edward II* and his untimely death robbed English literature of a major talent. In modern times, Stagecoach No. 19840, an ADL Enviro400, works towards Canada Water in early 2014.

The days of Rover SD1 police cars are now but a distant memory, revived occasionally by screenings of old movies and television programmes such as *Biggles* or *The Bill*. BMW alongside Ford, Hyundai, Peugeot, Vauxhall and others have been used by the Metropolitan Police in recent years. At Lewisham, a Metropolitan Police BMW shares road space with Go-Ahead London WVL 149 in 2014.

The London Borough of Lewisham includes the districts of Brockley, Catford, Deptford, Forest Hill, Hither Green, New Cross, Sydenham and parts of Blackheath. The focal point of the borough is Lewisham, a major shopping district on the fringe of inner London. Stagecoach No. 19844 approaches the town centre bound for Grove Park during 2014.

E 214 is an ADL Enviro400 in service with Go-Ahead London General. Lewisham is situated on the River Ravensbourne, which becomes Deptford Creek towards the Thames. E 214 was pictured near the Lewisham Centre, opened in 1977. In the background various high-rise tower blocks represent a questionable addition to the local townscape.

Distinctive Optare Olympus bodywork is carried by Metrobus No. 874, a Scania OmniCity N230 UD. Scania Metropolitans were operated in the late 1970s around south-east London. Handsome, fast and popular with passengers, the Metropolitans suffered reliability and corrosion problems. Classed MD, they entered service at New Cross and Peckham in 1975 but all had been withdrawn by 1983. Lewisham, 2014.

A trio of buses outside the Lewisham Centre led by DWL 26, a Wright-bodied VDL Bus SB120 in service with Go-Ahead London General. VDL Bus & Coach is based at Valkenswaard, Netherlands, and is an amalgamation of various bus manufacturers, the best known being DAF, Berkhof, Bova and Jonckheere. The SB120 was originally a DAF product launched in 1999 and popular with Arriva.

Metrobus No. 605 is a 2006 Scania OmniTown/East Lancs Myllennium combination photographed at Lewisham. East Lancashire Coachbuilders of Blackburn were founded in 1934, their rather utilitarian designs being popular with municipal operators including Blackpool, Brighton, Lancaster and Rossendale. The company was acquired by the Darwen Group in 2007 but by 2008 had been subsumed into Leeds-based Optare (itself connected to the Darwen Group). The last East Lancs bodies were constructed in 2011 before the closure of the Blackburn works in 2012.

Buses in Greater London

On the A21 High Street, Stagecoach No. 18481 passes Lewisham fire station en route to Bellingham (Catford Bus Garage). The busy and often tiresome A21 connects Lewisham with Hastings. After a dispiriting slog through Catford, the road continues to Bromley, Sevenoaks, Royal Tunbridge Wells and on into Sussex. The oldest section of the road between Sevenoaks and Royal Tunbridge Wells was opened in 1710 as a turnpike road.

A prospective passenger hails a Brixton-bound Transbus Dart/Transbus Pointer combination at Lewisham in 2014. Lewisham was a Kent town until the creation of the London County Council in 1889. People from the western side of Kent were traditionally known as Kentish Men, those from the east, Men of Kent.

Catford is the location of MetroBus No. 904, an East Lancs-bodied Scania N94 UD new in 2006. The Excalibur Estate in Catford is an interesting example of a post-war prefabricated estate. In 1945–6, 189 houses were constructed as a low-cost solution to Catford's housing crisis. Six properties were Grade II listed in 2009 before the majority of the houses were demolished, ironically to make way for new flats to help ease the housing crisis in Lewisham.

Representing the Royal Borough of Greenwich is Shooters Hill to the south of Woolwich. SE 55, an ADL Dart 4/ADL Enviro200 combination, works along Shooters Hill, the former Roman road known as Watling Street. A surprisingly green and sylvan part of south-east London, Shooters Hill summit stands at 432 feet above the surrounding suburbs, which include Eltham and Falconwood.

A trio of Go-Ahead London buses at Shooters Hill, with E 238, SE 55 and, facing the camera, E 43 in view. The Shooters Hill section of Watling Street connected London with the ports of Dubris (Dover), Rutupiae (Richborough), Lemanis (Lympne) and Regulbium (Reculver), now in Kent. Other sections of Watling Street pass through the boroughs of Westminster, Barnet, Brent, Camden and Harrow on the route to Verulamium (St Albans) and Viroconium Cornoviorum (Wroxeter).

Falconwood is a pleasant, neatly planned 1930s housing estate situated between the old Watling Street and more modern Rochester Way. The estate was built by Ideal Homesteads and is a good example of London's interwar suburban housing. Go Ahead London General SE 76 was pictured on service B16 to Bexleyheath, the principal town in the London Borough of Bexley. Falconwood, 2014.

The London Borough of Bexley is predominantly suburban in character, especially around Welling, Bexley, Bexleyheath and Sidcup. The district becomes more industrial around Erith and distinctly dystopian around the Bexley portion of Thamesmead, a brutalist post-war estate made famous in the 1971 film *A Clockwork Orange*. Go-Ahead London SE 73, an ADL Dart 4/ADL Enviro200, was pictured traversing the housing estates of Welling in the summer of 2014.

The sleek lines of this Plaxton President-bodied Volvo B7TL can be seen in this 2014 view from Erith, a riverside town on the fringe of London. No. 86 was new in 2000 and was being used as a driver trainer bus. Probably the most demanding place to drive a PCV in England, London's bus companies are constantly advertising for new staff as turnover rates remain stubbornly high.

Arriva No. 4029 was on conventional bus duties when photographed at Erith in 2014. Erith is the industrial end of Bexley; the town fronts the River Thames and stands opposite a huge landfill site near Wennington Marshes. Granted a market charter in 1315, Erith was briefly a resort town like nearby Gravesend, but the character of the town was ultimately determined by the docks and associated industries rather than tourism.

Bromley is the biggest borough in terms of land area. Stretching from Chislehurst and Crystal Palace to the North Downs, the borough includes the old and much expanded town of Bromley and the stereotypical Conservative commuter town of Orpington. MetroBus No. 904 was photographed at Bromley Common in 2014.

Metrobus No. 913, an East Lancs-bodied Scania N94 UD, traverses the typically leafy streets around Hayes en route for Ramsden Estate, Orpington. The now demolished Hayes Place was the home of William Pitt the Elder and his son William Pitt the Younger. This Hayes should not be confused with Hayes, Middlesex, a part of London with a distinctly industrial character. Hayes, 2014.

On the edge of Orpington, Farnborough retains a more rural ambience due in part to the attractive High Elms Country Park. Metrobus No. 517 is an all-Scania product known as the OmniCity CN94 UB.

Deep in south London's rural-urban fringe is Leaves Green, a hamlet situated between Keston and Biggin Hill. Metrobus No. 462 is another East Lancs-bodied Scania N94UD, a type popular in the fleet at the time. Leaves Green, summer 2014.

No. 462 was pictured on another occasion in 2014 at the bottom of Biggin Hill Valley. Service 320 connects semi-rural Biggin Hill with the decidedly urban Catford. The Surrey and Kent border is a short distance away and Biggin Hill carries a Westerham (TN16) postcode despite being officially part of London since 1965.

Metrobus No. 977 is a Scania OmniCity N230UD, pictured climbing up Stock Hill at Biggin Hill during 2014. The last of these distinctive buses was assembled in 2012. RAF Biggin Hill was a key fighter base during the Battle of Britain in 1940. The late Revd Gerald Flood was a popular Catholic priest who served Biggin Hill for over thirty years before his retirement in 2018 and death in 2020.

The London Borough of Croydon stretches from Norbury, Norwood and Thornton Heath all the way down to suburban Coulsdon, New Addington, Purley and Selsdon. The heart of the borough is, however, Croydon, transformed from a Surrey market town into a British version of an American city – complete with flyovers and endless high-rise office blocks. In typical Croydon surrounding, a variety of red London buses compete for the eye in this 2014 picture.

Opinions about Croydon's architecture tend towards the negative. A variety of tower blocks dominate the more humane scale of Croydon's Friends Meeting House in this 2014 view of London General's DOE 27, an Optare Olympus-bodied ADL Trident 2.

Bland and functional post-war architecture dominates London General's Wright-bodied Volvo B7TL, WVL 235 in central Croydon. The town has two busy railway stations named East Croydon and West Croydon respectively.

A quartet of double-deckers at Fairfield Halls, Croydon, in early 2014 with T 134 closest to the camera. The origins of Croydon's office-block development can be traced back to the Croydon Corporation Act 1956, a plan designed to lure big business from central London. Croydon is about 12 miles from the City of London and very close to some of Surrey's wealthiest towns and villages.

The much rebuilt Croydon streetscape can be seen in this view of Arriva DW 99, a Wright-bodied VDL Bus DB250 bound for Warlingham in the Tandridge district of Surrey.

The handsome but angular lines of the ADL Trident 2/ADL Enviro400 body are shown in this view of Arriva T 137 at Croydon. The lack of destination information on routes such as the 250 have been criticised by passengers and enthusiasts alike. Croydon, 2014.

A fine pair at Croydon, with Metrobus No. 451, an East Lancs-bodied Scania N94UD OmniDekka, setting down at Park Street. On the left, Arriva VLA 155, a Volvo B7TL/ADL ALX400 combination, is heading to Stockwell, almost but not quite in central London.

ADL Enviro400 T 42 passes Wright-bodied DAF DB250 DW 28 at Purley. Coulsdon and Purley Urban District was formed in 1915 and abolished in 1965, following the formation of Greater London. Purley, 2014.

Many double-deckers carry a shield on the upper deck to prevent damage from overhanging trees. Marring the appearance of MetroBus No. 921, an East Lancs-bodied Scania N94UD, the barrier can be seen in this 2014 view from Coulsdon. No. 921 was working service 405 to Redhill, Surrey.

Semi-detached interwar houses form the backdrop of many outer London suburbs. Amid such a background, Metrobus No. 191 is seen at Coulsdon in 2014.

The urban jungle which constitutes the London Borough of Croydon has semi-rural patches. About as far south as one can go in London, an unidentified Arriva Enviro400 crosses Coulsdon Common in 2014. The Surrey boundary is out of view on the right.

A rare 1978 Vauxhall Viva 1300L estate car was attracting interest at Old Coulsdon in 2014. The HC Viva was the last Vauxhall to be produced in the UK without interference from General Motors' Opel division in Germany. Most Vivas were built at Ellesmere Port in Cheshire, the last models leaving the plant in 1979. Arriva T 51, an ADL Trident 2/ADL Enviro400 combination, heads south for Streatham. Old Coulsdon, 2014.

Moving from the edge of south London to east London, we arrive at Aldgate, which is thought to be derived from 'Old Gate'. The original gate formed part of the defences around the City of London. In modern times, Abellio No. 9461 and Arriva T 69 are pictured in heavy traffic crossing from Whitechapel High Street (Tower Hamlets) into the City of London at Aldgate High Street. Aldgate, 2014.

Whitechapel is the location for Tower Transit VN 36130 at work on service 25. The 25 connects Oxford Circus with Ilford via a long trawl through the East End. One of the capital's busiest routes, the unpopular Mercedes-Benz Citaro articulated buses were used on the route for several years. Whitechapel is a focal point for London's substantial Bangladeshi community. There is also a significant Bangladeshi diaspora in Saudi Arabia, Malaysia, Canada, Italy and the United States.

Tower Hamlets is the definitive East End borough. It was formed in 1965 from the boroughs of Bethnal Green, Poplar and Stepney, which were historically in Middlesex. Devastated by bombing in the Second World War, the borough has been progressively reconstructed. Tower Transit DN 33795, an ADL Enviro400, calls at Mile End Road in 2014, bound for Clapton. Wat Tyler rallied his followers at Mile End during the Peasants' Revolt of 1381.

Pausing at traffic lights in Bow is Stagecoach No. 17743. Bow was part of the Metropolitan Borough of Poplar between 1900 and 1965. Parts of Bow have become fashionable in recent years, a trend accelerated by the Olympic Games at Stratford in 2012.

A smartly painted pair of Wright-bodied Volvo B9TLs at Bow, bound for Ilford during 2014. Despite a world-famous business district centred on Canary Wharf, Tower Hamlets is one of London's most deprived boroughs.

Bow Church, the oldest building in the locality, is almost hidden by trees as Docklands Buses SE 141 and Stagecoach No. 15102 traverse Bow Road in mid-2014. Bow Church was badly damaged during the Blitz but thankfully survives on an island location at Bow Road.

One of the less common body types in London during 2014 was the MCV Evolution. Married to an Alexander Dennis Dart chassis, London Central ED 1 was heading for Lewisham when pictured at Bow Bridge. The MCV Company was formed from the ashes of Marshall of Cambridge in 2002.

Modern tower blocks form a backdrop to Stagecoach No. 17550 as it approaches Bow Interchange in 2014. The interchange forms an access point for traffic heading towards the Blackwall Tunnel or the A12 East Cross Route towards Essex.

Sober looking local authority flats provide a backdrop for VN 36115, a Wright-bodied Volvo B9TL operated by Tower Transit. A short-lived venture, Tower Transit was formed in June 2013 by Transit Systems. In June 2021 the west London operations passed to a new company called RATP Dev Transit London. The east London depot passed to Stagecoach the following June. Bow, 2014.

A rear-view picture of a Go-Ahead London ADL Dart 4/Enviro400, SE 149, at Bow Interchange during unsettled weather in 2014. The flyover can be seen on the right and a clearly defined cycle path, now de rigueur in London, on the left. The area forms the boundary between Tower Hamlets and Newham.

The London Borough of Newham is one of a number of districts in the capital with a 'majority minority' population. One of the borough's chief shopping districts is Stratford, an Essex town until 1965 and location of Stagecoach No. 17769.

The multiracial composition of Newham is visible in this photograph of Stagecoach No. 18271. An ADL Trident/ADL ALX400 combination new in 2005, it was pictured at Stratford during 2014. Stratford was originally known as Stratford Langthorne in reference to Langthorne Abbey on the bank of the River Lee (Lea).

A trio of double-deckers at Stratford town centre in 2014. From left to right are Stagecoach No. 17925, Tower Transit VN 36117 and Stagecoach No. 17535. Stratford achieved international recognition when it was selected to host the 2012 Summer Olympic Games. The Olympic Park, later known as Queen Elizabeth Olympic Park, was constructed over an area taking in Stratford, Leyton, Old Ford and Hackney Wick.

One of the smaller buses traversing Stratford in the summer of 2014 was Tower Transit's DMV 44223, a 2012 ADL Enviro200. Mixed-use developments to the north of Stratford town centre, around the Queen Elizabeth Olympic Park, are in a new area called Stratford City. Stratford station has been joined by a new station called Stratford International, although no trains currently enter the complex from abroad.

Working towards Manor Park, Stagecoach Enviro400 No. 10103 was pictured near Aldworth Road on a humid day in 2014. A broad range of ethnic groups and religions are visible in Stratford with Christianity and Islam being the dominant faiths.

Stratford's old bus station was a stark and blustery building with a multistorey car park built above it. The new Stratford bus station was designed to emphasise the importance of Stratford as a dynamic, modern transport hub. Apart from buses, Stratford is connected to the Docklands Light Railway, London Overground, London Underground and National Rail services. At least seven Stagecoach buses can be seen in this 2014 photograph at Stratford bus station.

London General WVL 199, a Wrightbus-bodied Volvo B7TL, presents a handsome sight at Stratford in mid-2014. The famous Eastern Counties Railway works was opened by George Hudson at Stratford New Town in 1847. The works closed in 1991.

Stagecoach No. 17588 is seen at New Plaistow Road heading towards West Ham Lane in a rather stark corner of Stratford during 2014. Following the creation of Greater London in 1965, the name Newham was chosen for this area to avoid giving prominence to the former county boroughs of East Ham and West Ham. Stratford was traditionally part of West Ham.

Cycle lanes are one of the most controversial features of the current transport scene in London. Do they worsen pollution by slowing down traffic? Or do they reduce pollution by increasing the use of bicycles? The debate rages on. Tower Transit VN 36149 traverses High Street, Stratford, bound for Oxford Circus with an unmistakable but incomplete cycle lane visible on the right.

The London Borough of Hackney has all the stereotypical characteristics of inner London, including high-density housing estates and stark contrasts between poverty and wealth. At Hackney Central, Arriva DW 222, a Wright-bodied VDL Bus DB300, new in 2009, works south en route for Victoria with St Augustine's Tower in the background.

At the same location, Arriva VLW 175, a Wright-bodied Volvo B7TL, sets out from Clapton depot bound for Euston in mid-2014. The London Borough of Hackney includes numerous settlements, the boundaries of which are often hard to define; these include Clapton, De Beauvoir Town, Hoxton, Homerton, Lea Bridge, Shoreditch and Stoke Newington.

Architecturally, Hackney is a mix of the old and new, a legacy of the Blitz and insensitive rebuilding projects. Several unsuccessful post-war housing developments, including the Nightingale Estate, have been cleared but much of the more recent housing is mediocre at best. Stagecoach No. 17873 sets out for Whipps Cross, past Arriva DW 251, in mid-2014.

Plenty of buses on view in this photograph at Hackney during mid-2014. Arriva's smart Wright-bodied VDL DB300 leads the group on service 106 to Whitechapel. Hackney has excellent transport links, perhaps a key factor in the renaissance of the district. There are several railway stations within close proximity, including Hackney Downs, Hackney Central and London Fields.

Arriva's DW 532 shown above has just cleared the Hackney Central railway bridge at Mare Street in mid-2014. The line forms part of the London Overground network created in 2007. The rolling stock is characterised by a smart white, blue and orange livery. Destinations served by London Overground include Barking, Chingford, Enfield, Richmond, Watford and West Croydon.

Pictured at Mare Street, Hackney, is Arriva LT 5, a New Routemaster built by Wright and first registered in July 2012. Other names for the class have included the New Bus for London, Borismaster and Boris Bus. Production of the New Routemaster began in 2011 and ended in 2017, following the launch of the unsuccessful Wright SRM in 2016.

A trio of Wright-bodied double-deckers, including VLW 128, at Hackney during mid-2014. Wrightbus, usually known as Wright, was founded in 1946 and named Robert Wright & Son Coachbuilders. Bus bodywork was produced from 1978, and by the 1990s Wright was a key player in the industry. The Ballymena firm went into administration in October 2019 and is now owned by Jo Bamford, heir to JCB of Staffordshire.

Arriva DW 210 and DW 207 form a fine pair at Hackney during 2014. Between the seventeenth and mid-nineteenth centuries, Hackney was a favoured residential district for London's aristocrats and merchants. The arrival of the railways and expansion of industry changed the character of Hackney, bringing with it poverty and in places substandard housing.

Arriva VLW 128 and DW 522 represent contrasting styles of Wright bodywork at Hackney. VLW 128, a Volvo B7TL, dates from February 2003. Sister bus DW 522 dates from April 2013 and is a semi-integral Wright Pulsar Gemini 2, built from VDL components.

The Trelawney Estate is the location for Docklands Buses SE 108. An ADL Enviro200, it was working service 276 to Stoke Newington. Docklands Buses was acquired by the Go-Ahead Group in 2006.

Arriva DW 426 calls at Kingsland High Street amid the usual traffic congestion and crowded pavements. The famous Ridley Road market at Dalston is a nearby attraction with stalls selling commodities and food from around the world. Dalston Kingsland, 2014.

The London Borough of Brent is a large borough in north-west London formed as a consequence of the controversial merger of Wembley and Willesden in 1965. A rather lonely turning circle at Stonebridge Park plays host to an unidentified London United ADL Enviro200. The notorious Stonebridge Park estate has now been demolished. Home to over 1,700 residents, the estate, built in the 1960s, was infamous for drugs, gun crime and antisocial behaviour.

Service 18 connects Euston with suburban Sudbury via Harlesden and Wembley. At Harrow Road, near Stonebridge Park station and close to the thunderous traffic of the North Circular Road, Metroline VW 1874 collects a passenger for the northbound run to Sudbury. Stonebridge Park garage at Brentfield closed in August 1981.

Metroline VW 1866, a Wright Eclipse Gemini 2, was pictured at Harrow Road, Tokyngton, on the frequent service to Euston in 2014. The name Tokyngton is seldom used today for the area between Wembley Stadium and Stonebridge.

For a brief period of time Wembley was considered one of outer London's best shopping districts but the arrival of Brent Cross Shopping Centre in 1976 hastened the town's decline. Amid modern blocks, out of scale with the older Metroland style architecture, are TE 1988 and VW 1850 at High Road, Wembley, during 2014.

The cramped surroundings of Wembley Central are shown here in 2014. A quartet of red buses, including VP 619 and VW 1179, make headway along the busy High Road. Wembley Central station was originally known as Sudbury. Wembley grew rapidly after 1911 and today with a population of over 100,000 it is one of London's most racially diverse districts.

A truly significant year associated with Wembley and embedded in English culture is 1966 – the year England won the World Cup. By pure coincidence, Metroline's DE 1966 was snapped at High Road, Wembley, bound for St Raphael's Estate at Neasden. Wembley, 2014.

Arriva No. 6100 was pictured in a gloomy Harrow bound for the busy Hertfordshire transport hub known as Watford Junction. Harrow comprises several subparts including Harrow-on-the-Hill, Harrow Weald, South Harrow, Wealdstone and West Harrow – practically all suburban and multicultural in character. Architecturally, Harrow is perhaps the epitome and epicentre of London's Metroland. Harrow, 2014.

The privatisation of London Buses brought in numerous bodybuilders hitherto rarely seen, if at all, in the capital. In 2014, Transdev London Sovereign was operating this East Lancs-bodied Volvo B7TL (VLE 34) at Harrow. East Lancs used their own idiosyncratic spellings at this time much to the chagrin of English specialists. VLE 34 is fitted with East Lancs upright Myllennium Vyking body.

Arriva No. 6109, a Volvo B7TL/ADL ALX400 combination, was captured in central Harrow on service 258 to South Harrow. The famous Harrow School, situated at the deceptively rural Harrow-on-the-Hill, was founded in 1572. Famous Harrovians include Lord Palmerston, Lord Byron and Sir Winston Churchill.

The London Borough of Ealing stretches from Acton in the east to Greenford, Northolt and Southall in the west. The epicentre of the borough is Ealing, which for decades styled itself 'the queen of the suburbs'. One of the boroughs more colourful districts is the town of Southall, location of Metroline DES 1711, an ADL Enviro200. Southall, 2014.

London United was a keen user of the Polish-built Scania OmniCity. SP 46 loads up in a quiet corner of Southall, bound for Hounslow, in mid-2014. Southall is affectionately known as 'Little India' due to a massive Indian and South Asian diaspora. Most of the initial immigrants were attracted to Southall by the availability of jobs, the proximity to Heathrow Airport and cheap housing.

The styling of the Scania OmniCity is slightly reminiscent of the Van Hool McArdle-bodied Volvo Ailsas delivered to South Yorkshire PTE in 1976/77. Ten of this batch later operated from London Buses' Potters Bar garage in Hertfordshire. New in 2010, SP 176 loads amid the hustle and bustle of The Broadway, Southall, in 2014.

Southall was home to the Associated Equipment Company (AEC), which was regrettably closed by British Leyland in 1979. Famous AEC products included the Regent, Reliance, Mercury and some Leyland Marathons. The plant was located at the rural sounding Windmill Lane, near the Grand Union Canal. Metroline No. 1560 works towards Hayes and Uxbridge in 2014.

Another Metroline ADL Enviro200, on this occasion working service 195 to Charville Lane Estate, Hayes, at South Road, Southall. Southall railway station was opened on 1 May 1839 by the Great Western Railway. Southall is one of a handful of English railway stations to have a bilingual platform sign, in this case Gurmukhi, a script used in the Punjabi language. Other bilingual English railway stations include Hereford (Welsh) and Wallsend (Latin).

Hounslow is a long, thin borough stretching from Chiswick to Feltham on the north bank of the River Thames. Hounslow has long been one of London's most diverse boroughs. As long ago as 1991, half the population of Hounslow West was from a BAME group, mainly from the Indian subcontinent. In 2014, London United SP 189, a 2010 Scania OmniCity, passes the shopping parade at Hounslow West bound for Southall.

The unrelieved red of London United's ADE 7, an ADL Enviro400, looks surprisingly effective in this 2014 view from Hounslow West. Besides Hounslow, the eponymous borough includes Chiswick, Cranford, Feltham, Hanworth and Isleworth, plus the former Middlesex county town of Brentford.

The sleek lines of the Mercedes-Benz Citaro are still impressive today. London United's MCL 1 was pictured at Bath Road, Hounslow West, in 2014. London United was founded in 1989 and privatised in 1994. Acquired by Transdev from London United's management in 1997, the company is currently part of the French-based RAPT Group.

London United's SP 173, a Scania OmniCity, battles through heavy traffic at Vicarage Farm Road, Heston, in 2014. On 30 September 1938, following the Munich Agreement, Neville Chamberlain gave his now infamous 'peace for our time' speech at Heston Airport. The site is now occupied by industrial units.

The London Borough of Hillingdon is a long, narrow district separating west London from Buckinghamshire, Hertfordshire and Spelthorne, a part of Middlesex now in Surrey. Many of the communities are suburban in character – Uxbridge, Ickenham, Northwood and Ruislip. There is also rural Harefield situated in the green belt abutting the M25, plus a number of villages dominated by Heathrow Airport – Longford and Sipson. Pictured in the industrial south of London's second biggest borough, at Hayes, is Metroline TP 1525, a Plaxton President-bodied Transbus Trident. Hayes, 2014.

The industrial town of Hayes, Middlesex, was famous for the production of vinyl records at EMI's Old Vinyl Factory. Other famous names still based at Hayes include Heinz and United Biscuits. Near the Clayton Road bus stop, Metroline DE 1585 prepares to work south towards Feltham. Hayes, 2014.

A final shot from Hayes, Middlesex, illustrating Metroline DE 1174. Out of shot is the busy Hayes & Harlington railway station, originally called plain Hayes. The locality should not be confused with the terminus of the Hayes (Mid-Kent) line, listed on timetables as Hayes (Kent), despite being in Greater London.

We now take a short diversion out of Greater London to see some exiled AEC Routemasters. At Melton Park, Norfolk AEC Routemaster RML 2321 was being used for a wedding party. Melton Park was a principal location in the 1970 film *The Go-Between*. Melton Constable, 2015.

A magnificent AEC Routemaster is RML 2338, in service with Wensleydale Omnibus of Northallerton. New to London Transport in 1965, it awaits a wedding party at St Mary's Church, Norton-on-Tees, on 17 June 2022.

A pair of Wright StreetDeck-bodied Volvo B5LHs call at Drayton Hall, West Drayton. Hillingdon was one of only four London boroughs to vote to leave the European Union in 2016. The others were Barking & Dagenham, Bexley and Sutton. The result was tight in Hounslow and Bromley too. In the City of London 3,312 voted to remain against 1,087 to leave! West Drayton, November 2022.

Harmondsworth was still in existence during November 2022 despite the threat of destruction by developments at Heathrow Airport. A village of some interest, the most important structure is the medieval Great Barn, the largest in Britain. Abellio No. 8897 passes the New Life Destiny Baptist Church bound for nearby Hayes. The village centre is out of view on the right. Harmondsworth, 10 November 2022.

North Hillingdon is suburban territory to the east of Uxbridge. The A40 Western Avenue thunders away in the background, although the present road follows a new route with Hillingdon underground station resting in an island of constant traffic. Metroline DE 1023 calls at Long Lane bound for Brunel University, Uxbridge, in November 2022.

Harefield is a large village amid the green belt separating Buckinghamshire and Hertfordshire from suburban west London. HS2 railway developments pose a threat to the peace of this semi-rural haven. Metroline DEL 2153, an ADL Enviro200, was pictured turning into Breakspear Road North bound for Ruislip in November 2022.

Pictured at Rickmansworth Road, Harefield, is Abellio No. 8164, an ADL Enviro200 MMC. Harefield is the most westerly settlement in Greater London, about 17 miles from Charing Cross. Beyond Harefield is the commuter town of Rickmansworth, one of a small number of communities outside Greater London connected to the London Underground network, in this case the Metropolitan line.

Heston, Hillingdon Heath, Northolt, North Greenford, South Harrow and in this case Yeading form a cluster of amorphous suburbs in outer west London. RAPT Group BCE 47103, an electric ADL Enviro400 City EV, traverses Yeading Lane on the limited stop X140 towards Northolt and Harrow. The exotic sounding Food Bazaar on the left reflects the diverse ethnic profile of Yeading, an area of Hillingdon which was largely developed after the Second World War.

Situated perilously close to Heathrow Airport, Cranford's air permeates with the constant smell of aircraft fumes. Working out to Bull's Bridge, Abellio No. 8588 is seen opposite the Redwood Estate, Cranford, on a drab 10 November 2022.

A view from suburban Northolt in the London Borough of Ealing, showing Metroline's ADL Enviro400 TEH1452 at work on Ruislip Road. Northolt was known as Northala at the time of the Domesday Book (1086). The name is used today at Northala Fields on Western Avenue.

ADL (Alexander Dennis Limited) was formed following the collapse of Transbus International in 2004. Transbus had been created from the merger of two companies – Mayflower and Henlys in 2000. Mayflower owned Alexander (bodybuilders) and Dennis (chassis builders) while Henlys owned Plaxton. Here a London United ADL Enviro400 and ADL Enviro200, the antecedents of the Dennis Trident and Dennis Dart respectively, are pictured in Greenford during November 2022.

The relatively complicated modern history of Alexander, Dennis and Plaxton helps to explain why a chassis like the Dart or Trident can be badged Dennis, Transbus or ADL, depending on the year of manufacture. At Old Oak Lane, Park Royal, the modern successors of the Dennis Dart and Trident are illustrated on 11 November 2022. DE 1629 is a 2008 ADL Enviro200 and ADE 40444 is a 2012 ADL Enviro400. Park Royal, November 2022.

Commuters gather around Station Approach at the Hammersmith & Fulham section of Willesden Junction. Nearby Old Oak and Park Royal are being redeveloped in a plan to turn the area into the Canary Wharf of west London. Metroline DE 1629, an ADL Enviro200, was pictured on 11 November 2022.

Waiting time at the intriguingly named Scrubbs Lane, College Park, is London United ADE 40437, an ADL Enviro400. South of the Harrow Road, Scrubbs Lane is adjacent to Wormwood Scrubs Park and close to the fascinating but eerie Kensal Green Cemetery. College Park, 12 November 2022.

The Old Oak Estate at East Acton is a cottage estate built by the London County Council between 1912 and 1927. Now a conservation area, the houses have a fine period character. Similar in style is the Wormholt Estate to the south of the A40. On the Hammersmith & Fulham side of Old Oak Lane, London United DLE 30324, an ADL Enviro200 MMC EV, passes housing typical of the area in November 2022.

The Royal Borough of Kensington & Chelsea is home to many celebrities and millionaires who reside in elegant homes in fashionable districts such as Holland Park. At the less salubrious end of the borough is North Kensington, an area often featured in films and television shows such as *The Bill*. At Canal Way, London United BE 37038, an ADL Enviro200 MMC EV, prepares to enter Ladbroke Grove bound for Chiswick during November 2022.

A drab overall advert for Michael Kors mars the appearance of LT 955, a New Routemaster seen at Euston on 11 November 2022. Euston railway station is being redeveloped in anticipation of the opening of HS2 (High Speed 2), one of the most controversial infrastructure projects in recent times. Euston station is no stranger to controversy, the demolition of the original station in 1962 being described by the Royal Institute of British Architects as 'one of the greatest acts of Post-War architectural vandalism in Britain'.

People with an interest in the development of London's suburban architecture will find plenty of period styles to study in the northern reaches of Brent. Queensbury, a typical Metroland suburb, is a good example of the 1930s style. With the Tube station and shops as a backdrop, an unidentified Metroline Wright StreetDeck pauses at the crescent-shaped Queensbury Station Parade in November 2022.

Kingsbury has a diverse mix of domestic architecture and a typically stylish shopping parade at Kingsbury Road. Unfortunately, many Metroland shopping parades in outer north-west London, including Kingsbury, are underappreciated and in urgent need of restoration. RATP Group's ADL Enviro400 EV traverses Kingsbury during November 2022.

The much maligned suburb of Neasden is the location of Metroline VWH 2114, a Wright-bodied Volvo B5LH. The centre is an incoherent mess due to the monstrous North Circular Road, which isolates the shopping area from the Tube station and housing estates. The BAPS Shri Swaminarayan Mandir, better known as Neasden Hindu Temple, is a local landmark, and was for a brief period the biggest outside India. Neasden, November 2022.

In suburban Dollis Hill, Metroline VWH 2195, a Wright-bodied Volvo B5LH, works towards Oxgate and Brent Cross. The suburb was built around Dollis Hill House, the home of Lord Aberdeen, who frequently entertained William Ewart Gladstone. Dollis Hill House was demolished in 2012 and plans are afoot to rename Gladstone Park. Gladstone's father, Leith-born John Gladstone, was a slave trader and MP for Woodstock and later Berwick-upon-Tweed. Dollis Hill, November 2022.

A trio of Metroline Wright StreetDecks at the busy Pound Lane exit of Willesden garage. Our Lady of Willesden is one of many medieval shrines to the Virgin Mary in England. Pilgrims came to Willesden to venerate the image of the 'Black Madonna' and pray for intercession. The image was destroyed in 1538 at the peak of the Reformation. Today, Willesden remains a pilgrimage centre, although on a much smaller scale than Walsingham.

The confluence of three London boroughs at Willesden Junction might explain the shabby appearance of the locality. On the Brent side of Willesden Junction, usually reckoned to be Harlesden, an unidentified ADL Enviro400 calls at Station Road amid a large group of commuters and students. Willesden Junction, November 2022.

Kensal Rise in Brent has witnessed high levels of gentrification in recent decades, due in part to excellent transport links and close proximity to 'hip' areas such as Ladbroke Grove and Notting Hill. Metroline VWH 2409 descends Chamberlayne Road, scene of the 2006 tornado, en route for Trafalgar Square. Kensal Rise, November 2022.

The Watling Estate at Burnt Oak represents another large cottage estate built by the London County Council. With designed based on garden city principles, a total of 4,034 dwellings were constructed between 1924 and 1931. Crossing from the Barnet side of Watling Avenue onto the Harrow side of Burnt Oak Broadway, London Sovereign DE 20164 was pictured in November 2022. As a totality, Burnt Oak is usually considered a part of Edgware, regardless of the local authority.

The A5 is built upon the Roman road known as Watling Street. A rather grubby looking Volvo B5LH/Wright SRM combination, heads north on the Harrow side of Burnt Oak Broadway during November 2022. Service 142 connects Watford with Brent Cross via Edgware. Brent Cross Shopping Centre opened in 1976 and pioneered the concept of the out-of-town shopping centre in England.

Similar at first glance to the Wright SRM shown above, Arriva's New Routemaster (LT 1565) works through heavy traffic at West Green Road, Seven Sisters. A suburb of Tottenham, Seven Sisters was named after seven elms which were planted in the district and painted by John Greenwood in 1790. Tottenham, November 2022.

A trio of red buses at Walthamstow, principal town in the London Borough of Waltham Forest. Walthamstow was the birthplace of William Morris and visitors to the town today can visit the William Morris Gallery in Forest Road. Paul McCartney referenced Walthamstow in his 1979 punk song 'Old Siam Sir', a single lifted from Wings' swansong 'Back to the Egg'.

Walthamstow claims to have the longest street market in Europe. A key shopping and commercial centre for north-east London, Walthamstow was an Essex town until 1965. Waltham Forest Town Hall is a prominent building completed in 1942 and graced with Portland stone. At the modern bus station, opened in 2004, are at least eight buses in this November 2022 view.

Leytonstone was the scene of protests in the 1990s as environmentalists and residents attempted to stop the construction of the A12 East Cross Route. Close to the infamous road, a trio of double-deckers are pictured at rest in Leytonstone bus station during November 2022.

East Ham has a massive South Asian community, a fact reflected in colourful clothes shops and international grocery stores, not to mention the pungent smell of spices in the air. The London Sri Mahalakshmi Temple, just visible in this picture, provides a backdrop to Arriva ENL 73, an ADL Enviro200. East Ham, November 2022.

Barking is the principal town in the London Borough of Barking & Dagenham, although the latter town was excluded from the council name until 1980. Little of old Barking remains apart from the old abbey ruins. Amid the depressing architectural mess of central Barking are East London Transit LT 914 and Stagecoach No. 36282.

The epitome of white working class east London, Dagenham is a far more diverse place these days following the arrival of large numbers of West Africans and East Europeans from the late 1990s. Endless rows of council houses built by the London County Council are a key architectural feature of the area, with the massive Becontree development considered to be the largest council estate in Europe. A handsome ADL Enviro400 City EV, in service with Stagecoach, was snapped at Heathway, Dagenham, in November 2022.

A frequent sight around Greater London, Dial-a-Ride buses are used by residents with a permanent or long-term disability, such as blindness. At Dagenham, an unidentified Volkswagen T6 traverses Heathway. Several used Dial-a-Ride Volkswagens, with Bluebird Tucana coachwork, can be seen around England.

Havering is the third largest London borough by area, and one of the least typical in terms of population makeup – the population is overwhelmingly white and older than average. Pictured in Hornchurch is Stagecoach No. 19714, an ADL Enviro400, working service 252 to Collier Row. The key town in Havering is Romford, a community still psychologically part of Essex. Hornchurch, 11 November 2022.

The principal town in the London Borough of Redbridge is Ilford. Bus and Tube passengers arriving at suburban Newbury Park are greeted by this splendid but rather slender looking bus shelter, designed by Oliver Hill in 1937. Grade II listed in 1981, the shelter is 150 feet long and 30 feet high but was not actually constructed until after the Second World War. Stagecoach No. 36577 swings out of the shelter on 11 November 2022 bound for Romford.

Almost in the Epping Forest district of Essex, Hainault is a large housing estate on the edge of north-east London. The character of Hainault was determined by the London County Council, who constructed numerous houses there between 1947 and 1953. Stagecoach T 105 passes under the Central Line at New North Road en route for Chigwell Row, Essex. Hainault, November 2022.

The potential hazards of driving a bus are illustrated in this view from Tooting. Pedestrians, motorbikes, cars and tight streets provide challenging conditions for bus drivers at Longmead Road. Tooting is one of the key settlements in Wandsworth, a borough that also includes Battersea and Putney.

An impressive line up of red double-deckers at Morden in the London Borough of Merton. South London is not exactly abundant with Tube stations, Morden being the southern terminus point for the Northern Line. A distinctive but rather severe facade greets visitors to Morden underground station and is just out of view in this November 2022 picture.

No introduction is needed for Wimbledon. The invention of tennis is subject to debate, Walter Clopton Wingfield being recognized by many pundits as the modern founder of the sport in 1873. A trio of double-deckers are pictured at Wimbledon during January 2023. Go Ahead London's E 283 carries an unmistakable green livery for the University of Roehampton amid two standard red buses at Wimbledon Bridge.

The Royal Borough of Kingston upon Thames includes the eponymous town, Chessington, New Malden (home to a large Korean community) and the middle-class town of Surbiton, made famous in *The Good Life* (despite being shot in Northwood). Towards Chessington is the suburb of Hook, location of London United DLE 30067. An ADL Enviro200 MMC, it was seen working service K2 from Kingston Hospital to Hook on a miserable 12 January 2023.

A small, narrow wedge of Greater London containing Chessington and Malden Rushett cuts into Surrey between Epsom and Oxshott. Deep within the wedge, RATP Group BCE 47055, an ADL Enviro400EV, is seen on layover at Chessington World of Adventures. Nearby Chessington South station, opened in 1939, is the terminus of the Chessington branch line from London Waterloo. The section to Leatherhead via Malden Rushett was never completed.

The graceful frontage of Sutton station is marred by ugly tower blocks, out of scale with the traditional streetscape of the town. Historically a Surrey town, Sutton's growth can be traced back to the opening of the railway station in 1847. Photographed outside the station is SOE 10, an ADL Enviro200 Dart/Optare Esteem (East Lancs) combination operated by Go-Ahead London.

WS 41 is a Wright StreetLite working service S1 to Banstead. The StreetLite is an integral midibus available in two body styles and five body lengths. WS 41 is the short, wheel-forward type, known as the WF. Compare with the DF (door-forward) type illustrated at Cockfosters. Sutton, January 2023.

A row of pretty shopfronts brighten up the January gloom at Cheam Road, Sutton. An unidentified Go-Ahead London double-decker works the limited stop X26 from Heathrow Airport to West Croydon via Kingston. Sutton, January 2023.

There are two places called Belmont in Greater London, one at Harrow and another in Sutton, close to Banstead Downs. Pictured from Commonside Close, Banstead are a trio of red buses with Go-Ahead London's E 114 and WVN 40 closest to the camera. A RAPT ADL Enviro200 is visible in the background. The London–Surrey boundary is situated at Commonside Close. Belmont, January 2022.

Large office blocks are a feature of many Greater London railway stations, as is the case with Wallington, a town situated between Croydon and Sutton. Go-Ahead London's EH 227, an ADL Enviro400 MMC, was pictured on layover ahead of SOE 34 on 12 January 2023.

Cockfosters is situated at the beginning (or end) of the Piccadilly Line between Uxbridge/Rayners Lane or Heathrow Airport Terminal 4 or 5. Cockfosters is located in the London Borough of Enfield, a district which includes affluent suburbs, picturesque countryside around Enfield Chase, and industrial and impoverished districts such as Edmonton and Ponders End in the Lee Valley. Departing the small bus station at Cockfosters underground station is SL 92, a Wright StreetLite DF operated by Sullivan Buses of Hertfordshire.

The driver of AE 22 wipes his windows at a chilly Station Parade, Southgate, on 13 January 2023. Southgate underground station is one of Charles Holden's masterworks. Built in the art-deco style and opened in 1933, the complex was listed in 1971 and upgraded again in 2009. The circular, flying saucer exterior design and period lamp-posts provide a fantastic introduction to Southgate.

Tottenham Hale was once a detached part of Tottenham. Situated close to the River Lee and the long, narrow Lee Valley, Tottenham Hale is a mixture of industrial units and working class housing estates. Recent developments have included the construction of tower blocks, a retail park and a new bus station. Waiting under the canopy of the futuristic looking bus station, opened in 2014, are Arriva DW 470, a VDL DB300/Wright combination, and an unidentified Go-Ahead London New Routemaster. Tottenham Hale, January 2023.

Stroud Green Road, Finsbury Park, forms the boundary between the boroughs of Haringey and Islington. One of north London's edgier districts, Finsbury Park is a socially and ethnically diverse area named after the eponymous park, opened in 1869. On the Islington side of Finsbury Park, Metroline TE 1575 works service 210 to Brent Cross.

Finsbury Park Interchange is located next to the busy railway and underground station. A trio of red double-deckers are pictured on routes to Brent Cross, Northumberland Park (Tottenham) and Muswell Hill Broadway respectively in January 2023. At the time of writing, Finsbury Park was located in the Islington North parliamentary constituency, the smallest seat by area in the UK.

Liverpool Street station is named after the largely forgotten Conservative Prime Minister Lord Liverpool, who governed a troubled Great Britain between 1812 and 1827. Located within the City, the smallest and least populated London borough, the station serves east London and East Anglia. A trio of double-deckers led by Arriva HA 52, an ADL Enviro400H City, stand at Sun Street Passage in harsh January sunshine.

The unique Westbourne Park garage opened on 15 August 1981 utilising a tight space between the Grand Union Canal and a main-line railway on the fringe of the City of Westminster. The most interesting aspect of the garage is the use of the A40 Westway as part of the garage roof. OME 46010, an Optare Metrodecker EV, was pictured near the garage at Great Western Road in January 2023.

Emerging cautiously from the gloom of Westbourne Park garage is RAPT VDW 41003, a Wright-bodied Volvo B9TL. The roof carrying the elevated A40 Westway is clearly visible. The Westway was a highly controversial road scheme constructed between 1962 and 1970. Those living close to the road have suffered immensely from noise and engine pollution. Westbourne Park, January 2023.

White City is situated at the north end of Shepherd's Bush. The original White City was a sports and exhibition centre opened in 1908 to host the Olympic Games and Franco-British Exhibition. Metroline VMH 2581, a MCV EvoSeti-bodied Volvo B5LH, basks in the winter sun at White City bus station during January 2023.

On a dismal January morning, an unidentified Metroline Enviro400 calls outside the Hyde United Reform Church at Colindale bound for Kilburn Park. The area is historically associated with aeronautics and the Royal Air Force. The RAF, founded in 1918, owned Hendon Aerodrome, which later became the Grahame Park council housing estate in the 1970s.

Cricklewood is a somewhat ill-defined district on the on the edge of Barnet, Brent and Camden boroughs. Pictured on the neatly planned Golders Green Estate are Arriva SW1 and RAPT Group DDE 20291 at Pennine Drive. The estate was constructed on the site of Cricklewood Aerodrome, which closed in 1929. Cricklewood, January 2023.

Another picture from Pennine Drive NW2, illustrating Arriva's HV 188, a Wright-bodied Volvo B5LH. The style of bodywork is known as the Eclipse Gemini 3. Cricklewood was the scene of the 'Battle of Grunswick' in 1977. The industrial dispute centred on the attempt by female workers, mainly Asian, to join a trade union.

Alperton has undergone significant redevelopment in recent years with monstrous tower blocks rising around the Grand Union Canal near Ealing Road. Considered a part of Wembley, Alperton stands aside the River Brent and the constant roar of the North Circular Road. Pictured at Glacier Way, London Sovereign ADH 45284 represents the move towards hybrid power with this ADL Enviro400 MMC. Alperton, January 2023.

A typical Metroland suburb is Sudbury, home to two attractive Tube stations designed by Charles Holden – Sudbury Town and Sudbury Hill. Metroline's VWH 2139, a Wright-bodied Volvo B5LH, prepares to leave Harrow Road on service 92 to St Raphael's North. Sudbury, 14 January 2023.

A final picture from Ilford showing Arriva DW 238 departing Newbury Park.